Tofu Recipes

The Ultimate Tofu Cookbook

BY

April Blomgren

Copyright 2017 April Blomgren

License Notes

No part of this Book can be reproduced in any form or by any means including print, electronic, scanning or photocopying unless prior permission is granted by the author.

All ideas, suggestions and guidelines mentioned here are written for informative purposes. While the author has taken every possible step to ensure accuracy, all readers are advised to follow information at their own risk. The author cannot be held responsible for personal and/or commercial damages in case of misinterpreting and misunderstanding any part of this Book

Table of Contents

Introduction 6

Smoothies 9

    Tofu, Vegetable & Seeds Smoothie 10

    Tofu Fruit Smoothie 12

    Tofu Milkshake 14

    Strawberry, Banana & Tofu Smoothie 16

    Green Tea & Peach Smoothie 18

    Coffee, Banana & Tofu Smoothie 20

    Tofu Tropic Smoothie 22

Breakfast 24

    Tofu Tacos 25

    Scrambled Tofu 28

    Crustless Asparagus Quiche 30

    Tofu Pancakes 32

    Tofu & Vegetable Patties 34

    Tofu Omelet 36

    Frittata 38

Snack & Side Dishes 40

    Baked Garlic Tofu 41

    Fried Tofu 43

    Tofu Nuggets 45

    Tofu Pizza 48

    Tofu with Pak Choi 51

    Sesame Noodles with Tofu 54

    Tofu Wraps 57

Salad & Soups 60

    Baked Tofu & Broccoli Salad 61

    Curried Tofu Salad 64

    Glazed Tofu & Mushroom Salad 66

    Tofu Pasta Soup 69

    Hot and Sour Tofu Soup 72

    Tofu & Mushroom Miso Soup 75

    Coconut & Lime Tofu Soup 77

Main Course 79

    Honey-Ginger Tofu & Veggie Stir-fry 80

    Thai Coconut Curry Tofu 83

    Tofu in Chinese Garlic Sauce 85

    Vegan Fried Rice 88

Butter Tofu 91

　　Teriyaki Tofu 94

　　Tofu with Tomato-Mushroom Sauce 96

Desserts 98

　　Tofu Chocolate Mousse 99

　　Cinnamon French Tofu Sticks 101

　　Chocolate Peppermint Tofu Ice Cream 103

　　Chocolate Tofu Brownies 105

　　Tofu Peanut Butter Pie 107

Conclusion 109

Author's Afterthoughts 110

About the Author 111

Introduction

Tofu has been one of the key ingredients in South East Asian cuisines and commonly used in savory and sweet dishes. It is a product of soy milk which is prepared by boiling a grind mixture of soybeans. This is followed by coagulation of soy milk which results in curd and then pressing the curd forms the tofu cakes.

Due to its amazing quality to pair with any ingredient, and absorbing sauces, marinades, and spices, this versatile food can be used in any meal. Not only that, tofu is a perfect alternative to every kind of meat and fish.

With the promotion of vegetarian and vegan diet, tofu is widely used all around the world in every meal. Tofu is extremely healthy as it low in calories and abundant in protein, vitamins, calcium, magnesium, and iron. In traditional Chinese, tofu is considered for those who are slim, malnourished, and overweight and have high cholesterol and blood pressure and diabetes.

To master you with the cooking of tofu, in this cookbook we have gathered crazily delicious tofu recipes, from smoothies, to healthy breakfast, salads, soups, snacks, side dishes, main courses, and desserts.

Before you get started whipping up tofu dishes, let's have a look at the variety of tofu available in the market.

1. Extra soft tofu: Just like the name suggests, this type of tofu is softer compared to the other variety of tofu.

2. Soft tofu: Soft tofu is a smooth tofu which isn't drained and pressed. Therefore, this tofu contains a high content of moisture which needs to be squeezed from using in the cooking. Soft tofu is a great substitute for dairy products and thus, it is widely used in smoothies, milkshakes, and baking.

3. Firm tofu: Firm tofu is somewhat drained and pressed but still it contains moisture. Its firmness is similar to raw meat thus, it is a great substitute for meat. Eliminate moisture before using it.

4. Extra-firm tofu: In this variety of tofu, a large amount of moisture is eliminated. This tofu has the smoothness of cooked meat and its texture resembles that of cottage cheese. Use it or serve as you want, be it in cubes, strips or even in the form of noodles.

Smoothies

Tofu, Vegetable & Seeds Smoothie

This refreshing and energy boosting smoothie is packed with all the necessary nutrients and antioxidant to power you throughout the day.

Total Time: 5 minutes

Serving Size: 2

Ingredients:

- 1/3 cup silken tofu
- 4-ounce baby spinach leaves
- Half of a medium-sized avocado, peeled and pitted
- 1 medium-sized frozen banana
- 8 ounce frozen blueberries
- 4 ounce frozen strawberries
- 2 pitted dates
- 2-ounce walnuts
- 1 teaspoon hemp seeds
- 8 fluid ounce almond milk, unsweetened

Directions:

In a blender place all the ingredients. Pulse for 1 minute or until smooth and creamy, then pour into serving glasses and serve straight away.

Tofu Fruit Smoothie

This non-dairy and delicious smoothie is great for not only breakfast but also a powerful afternoon snack.

Total Time: 5 minutes

Serving Size: 1

Ingredients:

- 12.3-ounce silken tofu, drained
- 1 medium-sized fresh banana, peeled and sliced
- 8 ounce frozen mixed berries
- 1 tablespoon honey
- 4 fluid ounce grape juice

Directions:

In a blender place all the ingredients. Pulse for 1 minute or until smooth and creamy, then pour into serving glass and serve straight away.

Tofu Milkshake

Tofu milkshake is a wonderful addition to your everyday smoothies. It is incredibly creamy and super smooth without the use of any dairy item.

Total Time: 5 minutes

Serving Size: 1

Ingredients:

- 4-ounce soft tofu, drained
- 1 medium-sized frozen banana
- 1/2 tablespoon peanut butter
- 8 fluid ounce vanilla soy milk, unsweetened

Directions:

In a blender place all the ingredients. Pulse for 1 minute or until smooth and creamy, then pour into serving glass and serve straight away.

Strawberry, Banana & Tofu Smoothie

This smoothie recipe is a great way to keep you energized during the day. It just takes few minutes to make and can be paired with any fruit you might have at your home.

Total Time: 5 minutes

Serving Size: 2

Ingredients:

- 4-ounce silken tofu, drained
- 2 medium-sized fresh bananas, peeled
- 8-ounce sliced strawberries
- 1 teaspoon maple syrup
- 8 fluid ounce soy milk
- 4-ounce ice cubes

Directions:

Place tofu, bananas, and strawberries inside the blender and pulse for 1 minute or until smooth. Then gradually blend in milk until combined. Then add maple syrup and ice in the blender and pulse for another minute or until creamy. Then pour into serving glasses and serve straight away.

Green Tea & Peach Smoothie

Creamy avocado, peach and tofu smoothie is a new way to try green tea. This is an easy breakfast you have on the go.

Total Time: 5 minutes

Serving Size: 2

Ingredients:

- 2-ounce silken tofu, drained
- 8 ounce frozen sliced peaches
- 2 ounce frozen blueberries
- 1 medium-sized avocado, peeled and diced
- 1 teaspoon matcha tea powder
- 1 tablespoon chopped almonds
- 1 tablespoon shredded coconut
- 1 teaspoon hemp seeds
- 2 teaspoons maple syrup
- 8 fluid ounce coconut flavored milk, unsweetened

Directions:

In a blender place all the ingredients. Pulse for 2 minutes or until smooth and creamy, then pour into serving glasses and serve straight away.

Coffee, Banana & Tofu Smoothie

In this recipe, regular but delicious banana and tofu smoothie are present with a new twist and flavor of coffee. Have it as a breakfast smoothie, afternoon snack or evening drink if you want a boost of.

Total Time: 5 minutes

Serving Size: 1

Ingredients:

- 4-ounce silken tofu, drained
- 1 medium-sized frozen banana
- 1/8 teaspoon ground cinnamon
- 2 teaspoons instant coffee powder
- 1 tablespoon maple syrup
- 10 fluid ounce almond milk, unsweetened
- 1/4 cup ice cubes

Directions:

In a blender place all the ingredients except for cinnamon. Pulse for 2 minutes or until smooth and creamy. Then pour the smoothie into serving glass, sprinkle with cinnamon and serve straight away.

Tofu Tropic Smoothie

Brighten your day and enjoy all the tropic flavors at home with this amazingly refreshing smoothie.

Total Time: 5 minutes

Serving Size: 1

Ingredients:

- 6-ounce silken tofu, drained
- 2 cups diced frozen mango
- 1 teaspoon grated lime zest
- 2-ounce lime juice
- 12 fluid ounce pineapple juice

Directions:

In a blender place all the ingredients. Pulse for 1 minute or until smooth and creamy, then pour into serving glass and serve straight away.

Breakfast

Tofu Tacos

These breakfast tofu tacos are extremely easy to make as they are tasty. They are packed with protein and ready in less than 30 minutes, from start to finish.

Total Time: 25 minutes

Serving Size: 4

Ingredients:

- 12-ounce extra-firm tofu, drained and pressed for 30 minutes
- 1 cup baby spinach leaves
- 3/4 cup cherry tomatoes, sliced
- 1/4 teaspoon onion powder
- 1/4 teaspoon garlic powder
- 1/2 teaspoon ground turmeric
- 1/4 teaspoon taco seasoning
- 2 tablespoons nutritional yeast
- 1 tablespoon olive oil
- 1 teaspoon lime juice
- 2 tablespoons chopped cilantro
- 4 taco shells

Directions:

Place a medium-sized non-stick skillet pan over medium heat, add oil and let heat. Then add spinach leaves and cook for 3-5 minutes or until wilted. Remove spinach to a shallow dish and reserve pan. Place tofu into a bowl and crumble into small pieces. Add onion powder, garlic powder, turmeric, taco seasoning and yeast and stir until mix well. Return skillet to medium-high heat, add seasoned tofu and cook for 5 minutes or until cooked through. Assemble tacos by filling evenly with tofu and topping it with cooked spinach, tomatoes, cilantro and lime juice. Serve immediately.

Scrambled Tofu

15 minutes scrambled tofu is a savory and healthy option for a meal to start your day. It is quite easy to make and a quick substitute for scrambled eggs.

Total Time: 15 minutes

Serving Size: 2

Ingredients:

- 14-ounce extra-firm tofu, drained and pressed for 30 minutes
- 1 medium-sized red onion, peeled and chopped

- 1 small sized red bell pepper, stemmed, seeded and chopped
- 1/2 teaspoon minced garlic
- 2 tablespoons nutritional yeast
- 1/2 teaspoon onion powder
- 1/4 teaspoon garlic powder
- 1/2 teaspoon dried parsley
- 1 teaspoon salt
- 1/8 teaspoon ground turmeric
- 1/2 teaspoon Italian seasoning
- 2 teaspoons olive oil, divided

Directions:

Place a medium-sized non-stick skillet pan over medium-high heat, add 1 teaspoon oil and let heat until hot. Then add onion, garlic, pepper and sauté for 2-3 minutes or until onion begins to brown. Then transfer these veggies to a bowl and set aside until required, reserve the pan. Place tofu into a bowl and crumble into small pieces. Add remaining ingredients and stir until mixed well. Return pan to medium-high heat, add remaining 1 teaspoon oil and let heat until hot. Add seasoned tofu and cook until tofu begins to firm, stir every minute. Then add onion mixture and stir until just mix. Cook until heated through and serve.

Crustless Asparagus Quiche

This quiche is a great way to snack asparagus in your diet. It is very simple to make, just mix and bake.

Total Time: 30 minutes

Serving Size: 6

Ingredients:

- 14-ounce extra-firm tofu, drained and pressed for 30 minutes
- 7-ounce asparagus

- 1 medium-sized white onion, peeled and diced
- 14 fluid ounce soy milk
- 6-ounce all-purpose flour
- 1 tablespoon ground flaxseeds
- 1/2 teaspoon salt and more as needed
- 1/2 teaspoon ground black pepper and more as needed
- 1/2 teaspoon dried rosemary
- 4 tablespoons dill, chopped
- 2 teaspoons oil

Directions:

Set oven to 375 degrees F and let it preheat. Grease a small baking dish and set aside until required. Place tofu in a bowl and crumble into small pieces. Then mix in soy milk, and remaining ingredients, one after another, except for asparagus. Spoon tofu mixture into the prepared baking dish and spread evenly. Cut each asparagus in half and arrange over tofu mixture. Sprinkle with salt and black pepper and place baking dish into the oven. Bake for 20 minutes and then serve.

Tofu Pancakes

Fluffy tofu pancakes offer a nice hit of protein. It is too darn easy to make and perfect solution for egg pancakes.

Total Time: 25 minutes

Serving Size: 4

Ingredients:

- 2 cups all-purpose flour
- 16-ounce silken tofu, drained and pressed for 30 minutes

- 1/4 teaspoon salt
- 1 tablespoon baking powder
- 1 teaspoon ground cinnamon
- 2 tablespoons maple syrup
- 2 teaspoons vanilla extract
- 1/4 cup olive oil and more for frying
- 1 cup almond milk, unsweetened
- 1/2 cup cacao nibs

Directions:

Place flour in a bowl, add baking powder, salt, and cinnamon and stir until mix well, set aside until required. In a blender place tofu, add maple syrup, vanilla, oil and milk and pulse until combined. Then blend in flour mixture, 1-2 tablespoons at a time until semi-liquid batter come together. Place a medium-sized non-stick skillet pan over medium heat, add 2 tablespoons oil and let heat. Measure 1/4 cup of prepared pancake mixture and drop into the skillet pan. Sprinkle with cocoa and let cook for 5 minutes or until bottom begins to brown. Then gently flip the pancake and let cook for another 5 minutes or until nicely golden brown. Prepare remaining pancakes in the same manner and serve with maple syrup.

Tofu & Vegetable Patties

Tofu and vegetables patties are not only a go-to breakfast, but also a scrumptious lunch meal or side dish for the dinner. Feel free to pair your favorite vegetables with tofu and try your version of patties.

Total Time: 25 minutes

Serving Size: 8

Ingredients:

- 14-ounce extra-firm tofu, drained and pressed for 30 minutes
- 1 medium-sized carrot, peeled and grated
- 3 spring onions, peeled and sliced
- 1 teaspoon minced garlic
- ½ teaspoon grated garlic
- 2 eggs, beaten
- 2 tablespoon sesame oil
- 2 tablespoon olive oil

Directions:

Place all the ingredients except for sesame and olive oil in a large bowl and stir until mix well. Place a medium-sized non-stick skillet pan over medium heat, add sesame oil and olive oil and let heat. Take an 8cm cookie cutter, grease with oil and place in the pan. Pour prepared batter into the cookie cutter and let cook for 5 minutes until bottom is golden brown. Then carefully take off the cutter, flip the patty and let cook for another 5 minutes or until cooked through. Cook remaining patties in the same manner and serve warm.

Tofu Omelet

Tofu Omelet is a delicious translation of an egg omelet. The tofu provides sturdiness and the spices add tons of flavors.

Total Time: 55 minutes

Serving Size: 6

Ingredients:

- 12-ounce extra-firm tofu, drained and pressed for 30 minutes
- 1/2 teaspoon minced garlic
- 1 cup rolled oats

- 4 tablespoons sunflower seeds
- 2 tablespoons sesame seeds
- 3/4 teaspoon salt
- 1/2 teaspoon ground black pepper
- 1/2 teaspoon dried thyme
- 1/2 teaspoon dried tarragon
- 1/2 teaspoon dried marjoram
- 4 drops of Tabasco sauce
- 2 eggs
- 4 tablespoons tomato paste
- 1/2 cup shredded mozzarella cheese
- 4 tablespoons grated Parmesan cheese

Directions:

Set oven to 350 degrees F and let preheat. In the meantime, place all the ingredients in the food processor except for tomato paste and pulse until incorporated. Take a 9 by 5-inch loaf pan, grease the bottom and inner sides with oil and then spoon in prepared loaf mixture. Smooth the top using the spatula, drizzle with tomato paste and then place pan into the oven. Bake bread for 35-40 minutes or until top is nicely golden brown and inserted wooden skewers into the loaf comes out clean. Let baked bread cool in the pan for 10 minutes before turning out to cool completely. Slice to serve.

Frittata

The wonderful combination of potatoes, onions, and tofu makes a delicious frittata. They are perfect to serve for breakfast or brunch.

Total Time: 1 hour and 10 minutes

Serving Size: 6

Ingredients:

- 12-ounce extra-firm firm tofu, drained and pressed for 30 minutes
- 2 medium-sized potatoes, peeled and sliced

- 4 green onions, chopped
- 1 medium-sized white onion, chopped
- 2 teaspoons minced garlic
- 1 teaspoon salt
- 1/2 teaspoon ground black pepper, divided
- 4 tablespoons nutritional yeast
- 1/4 cup soy sauce
- 1/4 cup olive oil

Directions:

Set oven to 325 degrees F and let preheat. In the meantime, place a large non-stick frying pan over medium heat, add oil and let heat. Then add white and green onions, garlic and cook for 3 minutes or until vegetables begin to brown. Then add potatoes and season with salt and black pepper. Continue cooking for 12-15 minutes or until potatoes are nicely golden brown, stirring occasionally. In the meantime, place tofu in a food processor, add yeast and soy sauce and pulse until mixed well and thick. Spoon this mixture into a greased pie pan, top with cooked onion-potato mixture and place dish into the oven. Bake for 45 minutes or until top is golden brown and cooked through. Then immediately sprinkle with cheese and let rest until cheese melt completely. Slice to serve.

Snack & Side Dishes

Baked Garlic Tofu

Chinese-style baked tofu is super garlicky. It turns out great as a side dish in just 20 minutes.

Total Time: 20 minutes

Serving Size: 6

Ingredients:

- 14-ounce firm tofu, drained and pressed for 30 minutes
- 2 teaspoons minced garlic
- 1 teaspoon onion powder

- 1 1/2 tablespoon brown sugar
- 1/2 tablespoon cornstarch
- 2 tablespoons soy sauce
- 1 teaspoon Sriracha sauce
- 5 tablespoons water

Directions:

Set oven to 400 degrees F and let preheat. In the meantime, cut tofu into bite size pieces and place on a medium-sized baking sheet lined with a parchment sheet. Place the baking tray into the heated oven and bake for 40-45 minutes or until tofu is crispy and nicely golden brown, flip tofu halfway through. When the tofu is almost cooked through, place a small saucepan over medium heat and add remaining ingredients except for cornstarch and water. Whisk together cornstarch and water until combined and add to the saucepan. Bring the sauce to boil and stir frequently until sauce reach to desired thickness. Remove saucepan from the heat, add baked tofu and toss to coat. Serve immediately.

Fried Tofu

In this recipe, creamy mayonnaise and spicy Sriracha pairs well with tofu. This dish is a great and tasty alternative to French fries.

Total Time: 25 minutes

Serving Size: 24

Ingredients:

- 14 ounces of extra-firm tofu, drained and pressed for 30 minutes
- 1/2 teaspoon salt
- 1/3 cup cornstarch
- 1/3 cup mayonnaise
- 1/4 cup olive oil
- 1 tablespoon Sriracha

Directions:

Cut pressed tofu twenty-four sticks and dredge with cornstarch. Place a medium-sized non-stick skillet pan over medium heat, add oil and let heat. Add tofu and fry in batches for 5 minutes or until nicely golden brown. Transfer fried tofu pieces to a plate lined with paper towel to drain excess oil. Sprinkle with salt. Whisk together mayonnaise and Sriracha sauce and serve tofu sticks with it.

Tofu Nuggets

An alternative to chicken nuggets is tofu nuggets. These protein and vitamin packed nuggets are crunchy, cheesy and filling like the ones made with chicken.

Total Time: 1 hour and 10 minutes

Serving Size: 2

Ingredients:

- 16-ounce firm tofu, drained and pressed for 30 minutes
- 1/2 teaspoon minced garlic
- 1/2 teaspoon salt
- 1/4 teaspoon ground black pepper
- 1/2 teaspoon paprika
- 1/4 cup all-purpose flour
- 1 tablespoon nutritional yeast
- 1 cup whole almonds
- 1 egg, lightly beaten
- 2 tablespoons soy sauce
- 2 tablespoons olive oil

Directions:

Set oven to 400 degrees F and let preheat. Line a large baking with parchment sheet and set aside until required. Cut tofu into 1/2 inch thick squares and place in a shallow dish. In a bowl stir together garlic, oil and soy sauce until combined and then pour over tofu. Flip tofu until coat into the marinade and then place in the refrigerator for 30 minutes, flip every 10 minutes. In the meantime, place almonds in a food processor and pulse until coarsely ground. Add salt, pepper, paprika and yeast and pulse again until just mix. Place almond mixture in a plate, flour in another plate and egg in a separate bowl. Remove marinated tofu pieces from marinade, then coat with flour, dredge in egg, give a final coat of almond mixture and place on the prepared baking sheet. Coat remaining tofu pieces in the same manner and place on the baking sheet. Place the baking sheet into the oven and bake for 10-12 minutes or until nicely golden brown and toasted, flip halfway through. Serve immediately.

Tofu Pizza

Smoky and spicy tofu pizza features fluffy naan bread, spicy hoisin sauce, and juicy pineapples. Though the combination of pineapple and tofu seems weird, however, it tastes great.

Total Time: 55 minutes

Serving Size: 4

Ingredients:

- 14-ounce extra-firm tofu, drained and pressed for 30 minutes
- 2 naan loaves
- 8-ounce pineapple pieces
- 2 scallions, peeled and chopped
- 1 teaspoon minced garlic
- 2 tablespoons tomato paste
- 1 teaspoon liquid smoke
- 2-ounce hoisin sauce
- 4 tablespoons soy sauce, divided
- 4 tablespoons apple cider vinegar, divided
- 1 teaspoon Sriracha sauce
- 1 1/2 teaspoon maple syrup
- 4 fluid ounce water
- 2 tablespoons chopped cilantro

Directions:

Set oven to 400 degrees F and let preheat. Line a medium-sized baking tray with parchment sheet and set aside until required. Slice tofu into 1/2 inch squares. In a medium-sized bowl whisk together liquid smoke, 3 tablespoon soy sauce, 2 tablespoons apple cider vinegar and maple syrup until mixed well. Add tofu pieces and toss to coat. Arrange tofu pieces on the prepared baking sheet and place into the oven. Bake for 40 minutes or until tofu pieces are nicely golden brown, flip halfway through. While tofu bakes, line another medium-sized baking tray with parchment sheet and arrange pineapple pieces on it in a single layer. Place into the oven and bake for 20 minutes or until pineapples are tender. In the meantime, place a small saucepan over medium heat and add garlic, tomato paste, hoisin sauce, water and remaining soy sauce and vinegar. Stir until mix well and then bring to simmer. Then turn heat to low and continue simmering for 15 minutes, stirring occasionally. Place naan loaves on a baking tray and bake for 4-5 minutes or until hot. Then spread hoisin sauce over the top and layer with baked tofu pieces, pineapple, scallion, and cilantro. Slice to serve.

Tofu with Pak Choi

Sweet and sour tofu flavored with ginger and paired with Pak Choi is a healthy option for a meal. Even kids will love it.

Total Time: 30 minutes

Serving Size: 2

Ingredients:

- 8-ounce extra-firm tofu, drained and pressed
- 6-ounce Pak Choi, leaves separated
- 2 tablespoons grated ginger, divided
- 1/4 teaspoon salt
- 1/2 teaspoon dried chili flakes
- 1 tablespoon brown sugar
- 1 tablespoon apple cider vinegar
- 2 tablespoons and 1 teaspoon soy sauce
- 2 tablespoons olive oil

Directions:

Using a fork, prick holes into tofu and then cut into bite size pieces. In a large bowl stir together 1 tablespoon ginger, sugar and soy sauce until combined. Add tofu pieces, toss to coat and let marinate for 15 minutes. In the meantime, place a wok over high heat, add 1 tablespoon oil and let heat until smoking hot. Add remaining 1 tablespoon ginger and cook for 1-2 minutes or until fragrant. Then add Pak Choi leaves and stir-fry for 2 minutes. Add 1 tablespoon water and continue cooking for 2 minutes until leaves are wilted and stems are tender. Sprinkle with salt and divide Pak Choi evenly into two serving dishes. Wipe clean wok, add remaining 1 tablespoon oil and heat until smoking hot. Remove tofu pieces from the marinade and add to the wok, reserve the marinade. Stir-fry for 10 minutes or until nicely golden brown, stirring occasionally. Then add vinegar and reserved marinade and bring the sauce to simmer. Let sauce cook until it reduces to desired thickness. Sprinkle with red chili flakes and toss until mix well. Spoon tofu over Pak Choi and serve.

Sesame Noodles with Tofu

Give tofu an Asian influence by serving it with sesame noodles. It is very simple and needs just 10 minutes to come together.

Total Time: 10 minutes

Serving Size: 2

Ingredients:

- 8-ounce extra-firm tofu, drained and pressed
- 10-ounce egg noodle, cooked
- 5-ounce snow peas
- 5 ounce halved bok choy
- 1/2 teaspoon minced garlic
- 1/2 teaspoon grated ginger
- 1 tablespoon sesame seed
- 2 tablespoons soy sauce, divided
- 1 tablespoon and 1 teaspoon sesame oil and more for serving

Directions:

In a bowl stir together 1 tablespoon of each soy sauce and sesame oil. Cut tofu into 12 pieces, add to soy sauce mixture and toss to coat, set aside until required. Place a medium-sized wok over medium heat, add remaining 1 tablespoon oil and let heat until smoking hot. Add snow peas and bok choy, garlic, and ginger and stir-fry for 2 minutes or until vegetables begin to tender. Add 2 tablespoons water and continue cooking for another minute. Then add noodles along with sesame seeds and remaining 1 tablespoon soy sauce. Stir-fry for 2 minutes and then add tofu along with the marinade. Cover the wok and let heat for 1 minute. Then stir gently, divide evenly into serving plates, drizzle with sesame oil and serve immediately.

Tofu Wraps

The combination of crispy tofu with a scrumptious salad dressed in mayonnaise makes a crazily delicious and amazing wrap. Everyone who dislikes tofu will love this.

Total Time: 30 minutes

Serving Size: 4

Ingredients:

- 10-ounce extra-firm tofu, drained and pressed
- Half of medium-sized apple, cored and thinly sliced
- 4 large lettuce leaves, shredded
- 1/4 cup sliced celery
- 1 small red onion, peeled and sliced
- 1 teaspoon salt, divided
- 1 teaspoon ground black pepper, divided
- 2 tablespoons raisins
- 1/4 cup walnuts, toasted
- 2 tablespoons olive oil
- 4 teaspoons mustard paste
- 6 tablespoons mayonnaise
- 4 large wraps

Directions:

Cut tofu into 16 strips and set aside until required. In a bowl whisk together mayonnaise, mustard, ½ teaspoon of each salt and black pepper, set aside until required. In a separate bowl, place remaining ingredients except for wraps and oil, and toss to combine. Place a medium-sized skillet pan over medium heat, add oil and let heat until hot. Add tofu and season with remaining salt and black pepper. Stir-fry for 3-4 minutes per side or until nicely golden brown on all sides. When the tofu is done, remove the pan from the heat. Assemble wraps by placing wraps on a cleaning working space. Add prepared mayonnaise dressing to the salad and toss to coat. Divide this salad mixture evenly between the wraps and top with tofu pieces. Roll wraps, then cut each in half and serve.

Salad & Soups

Baked Tofu & Broccoli Salad

This salad bowl features an amazing combination of baked tofu, broccoli dressed in the delicious orange glaze. Though this salad needs time to prepare but it is worth the wait.

Total Time: 50 minutes

Serving Size: 4

Ingredients:

- 10-ounce extra-firm tofu, drained and pressed
- 1 1/2 cups broccoli florets
- 1 scallion, peeled and chopped
- 1 teaspoon garlic powder
- 3/4 teaspoon salt
- 1 tablespoon cornstarch
- 3 tablespoons soy sauce, divided
- 2 teaspoons Sriracha
- 3 tablespoon olive oil, divided
- 1/4 cup orange juice
- 1/4 cup crushed peanuts
- 1/4 cup chopped cilantro

Directions:

Set oven to 400 degrees F and let preheat. Cut pressed tofu into 1-inch pieces. In a large bowl whisk together garlic powder, salt, 1 tablespoon soy sauce and 1 tablespoon olive oil until combined. Then add tofu, toss to coat and let marinate for 5 minutes. Then sprinkle with cornstarch and toss. Line a medium-sized baking tray with parchment sheet, grease with non-stick cooking spray and then distribute marinated tofu pieces in a single layer. Take another medium-sized baking tray, line with parchment sheet, grease with non-stick cooking spray and distribute broccoli on it. Sprinkle with salt and place both baking trays into the oven. Bake for 30-35 minutes or until tofu is nicely golden brown and crispy on both sides and broccoli is bright green, flip tofu pieces and broccoli florets halfway. While broccoli and tofu bakes, prepare the glaze. Place a small saucepan on a low heat, add scallion, remaining soy sauce and olive oil, Sriracha, and orange juice and let simmer for 15 minutes, after 15 minutes of cooking, remove the pan from the heat and let rest until ready to serve. Assemble salad by placing baked tofu and broccoli florets in a bowl, add prepared glaze and toss to coat. Top with peanut and cilantro and serve immediately.

Curried Tofu Salad

This easy curried tofu salad takes just 20 minutes to come together, from start to finish. Make ahead in large quantity and serve at lunch for several days.

Total Time: 20 minutes

Serving Size: 4

Ingredients:

- 10 ounces extra-firm tofu, pressed and drained
- 1 small carrot, peeled and grated
- 1 stalk celery, chopped

- 2 tablespoons chopped white onion
- 1/2 teaspoon salt
- 1/2 teaspoon ground black pepper
- 1/8 teaspoon cayenne pepper
- 2 teaspoons sweet curry powder
- 2 tablespoons sliced almonds
- 2 tablespoons raisins
- 1/4 teaspoon maple syrup
- 3 tablespoons mayonnaise
- 1/2 teaspoon almond milk, unsweetened

Directions:

Cut tofu into 1/2 inch pieces and place in a medium-sized bowl. Add carrot, celery, onion, raisins, and almonds and stir until mix. In a separate medium-sized bowl place mayonnaise and whisk in cayenne pepper, curry powder, maple syrup, almond milk until combined. Pour this mixture over tofu mixture and stir until well combined. Then season with salt and black pepper and let chill in the refrigerator for 30 minutes before serving.

Glazed Tofu & Mushroom Salad

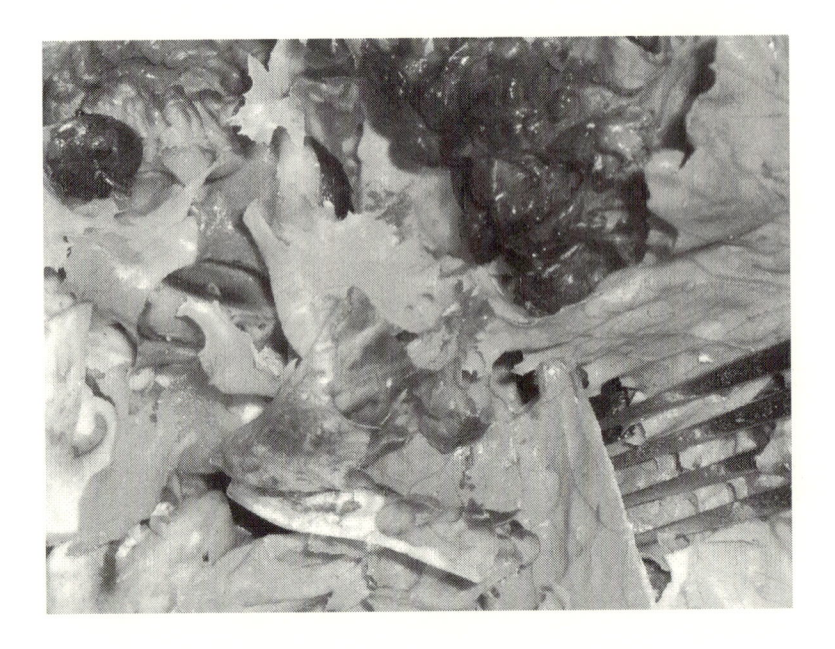

Japanese style tofu and mushroom salad is a vibrant and rich in taste and texture salad. Have it anytime of the day.

Total Time: 25 minutes

Serving Size: 4

Ingredients:

- 8-ounce extra-firm tofu, drained and pressed
- 1 cup mung bean sprouts
- 16-ounce shiitake mushrooms
- 1 scallion, peeled and sliced
- 2 medium-sized tomatoes, chopped
- 3/4 teaspoon salt
- 1/2 teaspoon ground black pepper
- 2 tablespoons soy sauce
- 1 tablespoon lemon juice
- 1/2 teaspoon sesame oil
- 2 tablespoons olive oil
- 1/4 cup ketchup

Directions:

Switch on the broiler and let heat until hot. In a small bowl whisk together soy sauce, sesame oil, and 1/4 cup ketchup until combined. In another bowl place 1 tablespoon of ketchup mixture, stir in lemon juice and set aside until required. Remove and discard mushrooms stem and then place mushroom caps on a baking tray, stem side down. Brush each mushroom cap with olive oil and then season with salt and black pepper. Place the baking tray in the broiler and broil for 4 minutes or until nicely brown, rotating halfway through. Then remove baking tray from the broiler, brush mushroom caps with prepared ketchup mixture and broil for another 30 seconds until crispy. Then turn over mushroom caps, brush with ketchup mixture and broil for another 30 seconds. Then slice mushroom caps into 1/4 inch strips, wipe clean baking tray. Cut tofu into 1/2 inch slices, brush with remaining ketchup mixture and place on the reserved baking tray. Return baking tray to the broiler and broil for 1 minute. After 1 minute, remove baking tray from the broiler and cut tofu slices into 1-inch cubes. In a bowl place sprouts, mushrooms, scallion, and tomatoes, add prepared ketchup-lemon mixture, season with salt and black pepper and toss until mix well. Add tofu pieces, toss lightly and serve immediately.

Tofu Pasta Soup

A tasty alternative to chicken pasta soup is this tofu pasta soup. It is very comforting and satisfying like the classic chicken soup.

Total Time: 45 minutes

Serving Size: 4

Ingredients:

- 8 ounces extra-firm tofu, drain and pressed
- 1 1/2 cups chopped carrots
- 1 1/2 cups chopped celery
- 1 cup chopped white onion
- 1 teaspoon minced garlic
- 1 teaspoon salt
- 1/2 teaspoon ground black pepper
- 1 teaspoon dried thyme
- 1 teaspoon dried parsley
- 1 tablespoon nutritional yeast
- 1 bay leaf
- 1 tablespoon soy sauce
- 1 tablespoon lemon juice
- 2 teaspoons olive oil, divided
- 6 cups vegetable broth
- 8 ounces whole-grain pasta

Directions:

Place a large non-stick skillet pan over medium-high heat, add oil 1 teaspoon oil and let heat until hot. Cut tofu into 1/2 inch cubes and add to pan. Cook for 5 minutes per side or until nicely golden brown and crispy. Transfer tofu pieces to a medium-sized bowl, add soy sauce and stir to evenly coat. Then sprinkle with yeast and stir until well combined, set aside until required. Place a large saucepan over medium heat, add remaining 1 teaspoon oil and let heat. Then add carrot, celery, onion, and garlic and let cook for 5 minutes or until onions begin to brown. Add black pepper, thyme, parsley, bay leaf and vegetable broth. Bring the mixture to boil and then reduce heat to medium-low heat. Add pasta and cook for 7-10 minutes or until the pasta is tender. Stir in tofu and lemon juice and continue cooking for 2-3 minutes or until heated through. Season with black pepper and salt, ladle soup into serving bowls and serve.

Hot and Sour Tofu Soup

This vegetarian soup is a great way to sneak in vegetables and tofu in your diet. It is a light in flavors and perfect to serve for the winter season.

Total Time: 60 minutes

Serving Size: 6 servings

Ingredients:

- 4 ounce sliced bamboo shoots, drained
- 0.5-ounce sliced mushroom caps
- 14-ounce extra-firm tofu, drained and pressed
- 1/2 cup sliced green onion tops
- 1 tablespoon grated ginger
- 1/2 teaspoon minced garlic
- 3/4 teaspoon ground white pepper
- 2 teaspoons white sugar
- 2 1/2 tablespoons cornstarch
- 2 tablespoons soy sauce
- 1/4 cup apple cider vinegar
- 32 fluid ounce chicken broth
- 12 fluid ounce water
- 1 egg, lightly beaten

Directions:

Pour water in a small saucepan, place pan over medium heat and bring to boil. Then remove the pan from the heat, add mushrooms in it and let stand for 30 minutes. After 30 minutes, add ginger, garlic, white pepper, sugar, soy sauce and vinegar and stir until just mix. Return saucepan from the heat and bring the mixture to boil. Then switch heat to low and simmer the mixture for 10 minutes, stir occasionally. In the meantime, whisk together 1/4 cup water and cornstarch until combined. Cut bamboo shoots into juliennes and add into simmering mixture along with cornstarch mixture and tofu. Switch flame to medium and bring the mixture to boil. Boil for 1 minute and then slowly drizzle egg in it, don't stir. Switch heat to low and continue cooking for 1 minute. Stir soup until well mixed, then garnish soup with green onion and ladle to serve.

Tofu & Mushroom Miso Soup

Enjoy super delicious miso broth paired with tofu and vegetables. It is perfect for a light and nutritious lunch or to provide warmth to the body on a chilly day.

Total Time: 15 minutes

Serving Size: 4

Ingredients:

- 6 ounces extra-firm tofu, drained and pressed
- 1/4 cup baby spinach leaves
- 4 ounces mushrooms, sliced
- 2 tablespoons chopped green onion
- 4 tablespoons miso paste
- 1 egg, lightly beaten
- 4 cups vegetable broth

Directions:

Place a large saucepan over medium heat, add broth and bring to boil. Cut tofu into cubes and add to the hot broth along with spinach and mushrooms and then slowly pour in egg, stir continuously. Cook for 2 minutes and then remove saucepan from the heat. Ladle out 1/2 cup of the broth in a bowl and stir in miso paste using a whisker. Pour this mixture into hot broth and stir until mix well. Garnish soup with green onions and ladle into serving bowls to serve.

Coconut & Lime Tofu Soup

This light and simple soup is perfect for everyone who doesn't have enough time to whip up a filling meal. Make a big batch of this soup and have it anytime in the week with some fruits.

Total Time: 30 minutes

Serving Size: 4

Ingredients:

- 14-ounce extra-firm tofu, drained and pressed
- 8-ounce button mushrooms, sliced
- 1 jalapeño pepper, de-seeded and thinly sliced
- 1 tablespoon grated ginger
- 2 teaspoons brown sugar
- 3 tablespoons soy sauce
- 6 tablespoons lime juice
- 13.5-ounce coconut milk, unsweetened
- 3 1/2 cups vegetable broth
- 3/4 cup cilantro leaves

Directions:

Place a large saucepan over high heat, add broth and bring the mixture to boil. Then switch heat to medium, cover the pan and simmer the broth for 10 minutes. After 10 minutes, stir in tofu, mushrooms, pepper and coconut milk and cook for 3 minutes or until mushrooms are tender. Add sugar, soy sauce, lime juice and ½ cup cilantro leaves and cook for 1 minute. Ladle soup into serving bowl, garnish with remaining cilantro leaves and serve immediately.

Main Course

Honey-Ginger Tofu & Veggie Stir-fry

The combination of tofu flavored with delicious honey-garlic sauce and vibrant vegetables is a vegetarian wonder. This healthy, nutty, filling dish will make your lunch or dinner exciting.

Total Time: 35 minutes

Serving Size: 6

Ingredients:

- 14 ounces extra-firm tofu, drained and pressed
- 2 cups cooked brown rice
- 2 cups chopped asparagus
- 2 cups shredded carrots
- 3 green onions, minced
- 3 garlic cloves, peeled
- 2 tablespoons grated ginger
- 1/2 cup soy sauce
- 2 tablespoons honey
- 1/4 cup apple cider vinegar
- 1/4 cup and 2 tablespoons olive oil
- 1/4 cup water

Directions:

In a food processor place garlic cloves and add ginger, soy sauce, vinegar, honey, ¼ cup olive oil, and water. Pulse until smooth and set aside until required. Place a large non-stick skillet pan over medium heat, add remaining oil and let heat. Cut tofu into small cubes and then add to the pan along with 1/4 cup of prepared garlic sauce. Stir-fry tofu for 7-10 minutes or until nicely golden brown on both sides. Remove tofu pieces to a plate lined with paper towels and set aside until required. Return skillet pan to medium heat and add asparagus along with ¼ cup of garlic sauce. Cook for 3-4 minutes or until asparagus is tender-crisp. Then add carrots and toss until mix. Serve these veggies and cooked tofu over rice, drizzle with garlic sauce, sprinkle with green onions and serve.

Thai Coconut Curry Tofu

If you are looking for a meal that comes together quickly with simple ingredients, then this recipe will end your search. Packed with bold and vibrant flavors and bursting with aromatic spices, this Thai coconut curry will tickle your taste buds.

Total Time: 30 minutes

Serving Size: 4

Ingredients:

- 14-ounce extra-firm tofu, drained and pressed

- 1 cup brown rice, cooked
- 1 teaspoon paprika
- 2 tablespoons red curry paste
- 1 tablespoon soy sauce
- 1 tablespoon maple syrup
- 1 tablespoon lime juice
- 3 tablespoons olive oil
- 8 fluid ounce coconut milk, unsweetened
- 1/4 cup chopped cilantro

Directions:

Place a large saucepan over medium-high heat, add oil and let heat until hot. Cut tofu into small cubes and add to saucepan. Cook for 3-4 minutes or until tofu cubes are nicely golden brown on all sides. Transfer tofu pieces to a plate lined with paper towels and set aside until required, reserve the pan. Switch flame to medium heat, add curry paste and coconut milk and stir until well combined. Switch heat to medium-high and simmer sauce for 5 minutes or until sauce reduced to desired thickness. Then reduce heat low and stir in paprika, soy sauce, lime juice until mix well. Return cooked tofu pieces to the pan and toss to coat. Cook for 1 minute or until heat through and then serve tofu over brown rice. Garnish with cilantro and serve.

Tofu in Chinese Garlic Sauce

In this version, Chinese-styled chicken in garlic sauce is present with a vegetarian twist. This quick dinner is a life saver on busy weekdays and weekends.

Total Time: 20 minutes

Serving Size: 6

Ingredients:

- 8-ounce extra-firm tofu, drained and pressed
- 1 medium-sized red bell pepper, de-seeded and sliced
- 2 medium-sized white onions, peeled and sliced
- 8 garlic cloves, peeled
- 1/2 tablespoons grated ginger
- 1 teaspoon salt, divided
- 1 teaspoon ground black pepper, divided
- 1 teaspoon red chili flakes
- 2 teaspoons cornstarch
- 1 teaspoon tomato Ketchup
- 1 tablespoon and 1 teaspoon soy sauce
- 1/2 tablespoon apple cider vinegar
- 2 tablespoons olive oil
- ¼ cup chopped cilantro

Directions:

Cut tofu into strips and add to a large bowl. Add 1 tablespoon oil, ½ teaspoon of each salt and black pepper, toss to coat and let marinate for 15 minutes. In the meantime, stir together cornstarch, soy sauce, vinegar and stir until mixed well, set aside until required. Place a large non-stick frying pan over high heat. Add remaining 1 tablespoon oil and place marinated tofu in the single layer. Cook for 2 minutes or until bottom is golden brown and crispy and then flip to cook the other side for 2 minutes. Transfer cooked tofu pieces to a plate lined with paper towel and cook remaining tofu pieces in the same manner. When the tofu pieces are cooked, add garlic, ginger and red pepper flakes in the pan, switch heat to low and cook for 15 seconds or until fragrant. Then switch flame to medium-high, add onions and cook for a minute. Then add pepper and continue cooking for 1 minute. Return cooked tofu strips to the pan along with prepared vinegar-soy sauce mixture, and toss to mix. Season with remaining salt and black pepper, then add 2 tablespoons water and cook for a minute or until sauce gets thick. Garnish with cilantro and serve.

Vegan Fried Rice

Though this version of fried rice takes more than 1 hour to come together but it is worth the wait due to its delicious taste. You will forget the take out version of fried rice once you have this.

Total Time: 1 hour and 15 minutes

Serving Size: 2

Ingredients:

- 8 ounces extra-firm tofu, drained and pressed
- 1 cup brown rice, cooked
- 1 cup chopped green onion
- 1 medium-sized carrot, peeled and grated
- 1/2 cup peas
- 2 1/2 teaspoons minced garlic, divided
- 3 tablespoons soy sauce
- 2 teaspoons chili garlic sauce
- 3 tablespoons maple syrup
- 1 tablespoon peanut butter

Directions:

Set oven to 400 degrees F and let preheat, take a large baking sheet, line with parchment sheets and set aside until required. Cut tofu into ¼ inch cubes and arrange on the prepared baking sheet in a single layer. Place the baking sheet into the oven and bake for 30 minutes or until nicely golden brown. In the meantime, whisk together 1/2 teaspoon minced garlic, peanut butter, soy sauce, chili garlic sauce and maple syrup until well combined. When the tofu is baked, add into the prepared peanut butter sauce, toss to coat and let marinate for 5 minutes, stirring occasionally. Then place a large non-stick skillet pan over medium heat and let heat. Remove tofu pieces from the marinade and add to the pan, and cook for 3-4 minutes per side or until nicely golden brown on all sides, stirring occasionally. Then remove tofu pieces from the pan to a plate lined with paper towels and set aside until required. Reserve the pan and add remaining 2 teaspoons minced garlic along with peas, carrots, and green onion. Cook for 3-4 minutes and then add 1 tablespoon soy sauce. Then add cooked rice and tofu, reserved marinade and stir until well mixed. Switch heat medium-high and cook for 4 minutes, stirring frequently. Serve immediately.

Butter Tofu

A vegetarian alternative to butter chicken is butter tofu. Soft tofu pairs well with the extremely flavorful and creamy spiced tomato sauce.

Total Time: 35 minutes

Serving Size: 6

Ingredients:

- 9 ounces extra-firm tofu, drained and pressed
- 2 medium-sized white onions, minced
- 15-ounce crushed tomatoes
- 3 tablespoons grated ginger
- 3 teaspoons minced garlic
- 1 teaspoon salt
- 2 tablespoons brown sugar
- 1 1/2 teaspoons garam masala
- 1 teaspoon ground turmeric
- 1 teaspoon ground coriander
- 1/4 teaspoon fenugreek seeds
- 2 tablespoons almond butter
- 1/4 cup olive oil
- 1/4 cup heavy cream

Directions:

Place a large non-stick skillet pan over medium-high heat, add oil and let heat until hot. Then add onion, salt and cook for 8-10 minutes or until onions are nicely golden brown. Add garlic, ginger and continue cooking for about 1 minute or until fragrant. Add garam masala, turmeric, coriander, fenugreek seeds and cook for 30 seconds, stirring occasionally. Switch heat to low, then add tomatoes along with ½ cup water and simmer for 15 minutes or until sauce thickens. Remove pan from the heat and let the sauce cool for few minutes. Transfer this mixture to a blender and pulse for 1 minute or until very smooth and return sauce to the skillet pan. Cut tofu into cubes and add the pan and place pan over low heat. Let cook or until tofu pieces are warm. Remove pan from the heat, add sugar, butter and cream and stir until mixed well. Season with salt and serve immediately.

Teriyaki Tofu

Crisped vegetarian version of teriyaki chicken is packed with a ton of flavors. Moreover, this quick dinner is very simple to make and required minimal efforts.

Total Time: 20 minutes

Serving Size: 4

Ingredients:

- 14-ounce extra-firm tofu, drained and pressed
- Half of a medium-sized red onion, peeled and diced
- 2 tablespoons brown sugar
- 2 tablespoons soy sauce
- 2 tablespoons sake
- 2 teaspoons apple cider vinegar
- 2 tablespoons olive oil
- 1/4 cup chopped cilantro

Directions:

Place a large non-stick skillet pan over high heat, add oil and let heat until hot. Cut tofu into 1-inch cubes and add to the pan in a single later. Cook for 3-4 minutes per side or until nicely golden brown. Then reduce heat to medium, add remaining ingredients into the pan except for cilantro and cook for 1 minute. Then remove the pan from the heat, garnish with cilantro and serve immediately.

Tofu with Tomato-Mushroom Sauce

This vegetarian curry is perfect to whip up for the busy weeknights. This light curry goes great with brown rice.

Total Time: 35 minutes

Serving Size: 2

Ingredients:

- 14 ounces extra-firm tofu, drained and pressed
- 1 ½ cups sliced mushrooms
- 2 medium-sized tomatoes, chopped
- 2 teaspoons olive oil
- 2 tablespoons green pesto
- 2 tablespoons crumbled feta cheese

Directions:

Place a large non-stick skillet pan over high heat, add oil and let heat until hot. Cut tofu into small cubes and add to the pan. Cook for 5 minutes per side or until nicely golden brown. Then add mushrooms and tomatoes and continue cooking for 2 minutes or until just cooked, stirring frequently. When vegetables are done, remove the pan from the pan, and stir in pesto and cheese. Serve immediately.

Desserts

Tofu Chocolate Mousse

One word for this dessert, heavenly! This chocolaty goodness tastes much better than the store-bought version.

Total Time: 40 minutes

Serving Size: 4

Ingredients:

- 3/4 cup and 2 tablespoons chocolate chips, divided
- 12 ounces silken tofu
- 1/2 cup milk, warmed

Directions:

Place 3/4 cup chocolate chips in a microwave ovenproof bowl and microwave for 30 seconds or until melted, stirring every 10 seconds. Then transfer melted chocolate to a blender, add tofu and pulse until puree. Then pour in milk and pulse until smooth. Pass this mixture through a fine sieve placed over a medium-sized bowl. Divide the mouse collected in the medium-sized bowl into four serving dishes and place in the refrigerator for 30 minutes or until chilled. Garnish with remaining 2 tablespoons chocolate chips and serve immediately.

Cinnamon French Tofu Sticks

Sweet and delicious French toast sticks is low in carb and amazingly healthy. It is a sweet treat for breakfast or dessert.

Total Time: 45 minutes

Serving Size: 3

Ingredients:

- 14-ounce extra-firm tofu, drained and pressed
- 1 tablespoon cocoa powder, unsweetened
- 4 tablespoons brown sugar
- 1 tablespoon ground cinnamon
- 2 tablespoons maple syrup
- 1 1/2 tablespoon coconut oil, melted

Directions:

In a small bowl stir together sugar and cinnamon until mixed well. Cut tofu into sticks and sprinkle with one-fourth mixture of the prepared cinnamon mixture. Place a large non-stick frying pan over low heat and let heat until hot. Add tofu sticks in a single layer and cook for 30 minutes, flip tofu strips every 4 minutes and sprinkle with one-fourth mixture of the prepared cinnamon mixture at each flip. When the tofu strips are almost cooked, prepared chocolate syrup. Place coconut oil in a microwave ovenproof bowl and microwave for 30 seconds. Then whisk in cocoa powder and maple syrup until mixed thoroughly. Drizzle this syrup over tofu sticks and serve immediately.

Chocolate Peppermint Tofu Ice Cream

This tofu ice cream is packed with amazing flavors of chocolate and refreshing peppermint. This ice cream is light without many calories.

Total Time: 3 hours and 15 minutes

Serving Size: 8

Ingredients:

- 16 ounces silken tofu
- 1/8 teaspoon salt
- 3/4 cup maple syrup
- 1/4 cup cocoa powder, unsweetened
- 1 tablespoon peppermint extract
- 1 tablespoon vanilla extract
- 4 fluid ounce almond milk, unsweetened
- 3 tablespoons coconut oil, melted

Directions:

Place all the ingredients in a food processor and pulse until smooth. Then transfer this mixture into a freezer bowl and place in refrigerator for 3 hours or more until thoroughly chilled. Pour this chilled mixture into an ice cream maker and process for 15 minutes or until the mixture resembles ice cream consistency.

Chocolate Tofu Brownies

Moist and low fat, these tofu brownies are wonderful. Everyone will love them and the kids won't stop eating.

Total Time: 30 minutes

Serving Size: 12

Ingredients:

- 8 ounces silken tofu
- 3/4 cup all-purpose flour
- 1 teaspoon vanilla extract
- 2 tablespoons corn starch
- 1/2 teaspoon baking soda
- 2 tablespoons water
- 1/4 teaspoon salt
- 3/4 cup white sugar
- 1/4 cup cocoa powder, unsweetened

Directions:

Set oven to 350 degrees F and let preheat until brownies are ready to bake. In the meantime, place tofu in a blender and pulse until smooth. Then transfer blended tofu into a large bowl, add cornstarch and baking soda and stir until mixed well. Then stir in flour, salt, sugar, cocoa powder, vanilla and water until incorporated. Take 8 by 8 brownie pan, grease with oil and then evenly pour the brownie batter into it. Place brownie pan into the oven and bake for 35 minutes or until cooked through and inserted a wooden skewer into the brownies come out clean. Let baked brownies cool in pan for 10 minutes before taking out to cool completely on the wire rack and then serve.

Tofu Peanut Butter Pie

Super easy and quick tofu peanut butter pie is absolutely lovely, decadent and yummy.

Total Time: 2 hours and 10 minutes

Serving Size: 6

Ingredients:

- 16 ounces silken tofu
- 8 fluid ounce peanut butter
- 3/4 cup white sugar
- 2 tablespoon soy milk, unsweetened
- 2 teaspoon vanilla extract
- 1 9-inch frozen pie crust, thawed

Directions:

Place all the ingredients except for pie crust in a blender. Pulse for 2 minutes or until smooth and then spoon this mixture into the pie crust. Place pie crust in the refrigerator for 2 hours or until set. Slice to serve.

Conclusion

Tofu is a breath of relief for every vegetarian who loves meat and fish. Furthermore, this versatile ingredient has many health benefits due to its nutritional value. It's well-known ability to pair with other ingredients and absorbing spices, marinade and sauces make cooking with tofu very easy.

The above-mentioned tofu recipes will not help you adjust to the vegetarian and vegan lifestyle but also use tofu correctly in the recipes. With the completion of this cookbook, you will master in cooking with tofu and will be able to use tofu in your daily cooking any way you want.

Author's Afterthoughts

Thanks ever so much to each of my cherished readers for investing the time to read this book!

I know you could have picked from many other books but you chose this one. So a big thanks for buying this book and reading all the way to the end.

If you enjoyed this book or received value from it, I'd like to ask you for a favor. Please take a few minutes to post an honest and heartfelt review on Amazon.com. Your support does make a difference and helps to benefit other people.

Thanks!

April Blomgren

About the Author

April Blomgren

Hello everyone! Are you ready to grill tonight? My name is April and I love to cook and entertain friends and family almost every weekend. If you share my passion for great food, easy preparation time but mouthwatering results, you and I are going to get along just fine!

I think a successful meal among loved ones is based on a few key factors: fresh ingredients and appropriate cooking method. Some meats for example, can truly benefit from being marinated overnight, and will be at their best prepared on the grill. Another aspect of cooking I must insist on, no matter what your cooking style is: rely on the use of herbs and spices. Please favor fresh herbs each time you can. However, I understand that it may be difficult during certain periods of the year, so simply keep a well-stocked pantry of dried basic herbs and spices such as cinnamon, nutmeg, basil, oregano, thyme or any other favorites.

Finally, once you embark that exciting culinary journey with me, you will realize that simplicity is also one of my allied. Don't overthink when cooking. Inspire yourself of recipes, have fun doing it and taste as you go. Sure, you might once in a while burn a few pork chops or use too much salt in your sauce, you are just human. Cooking is not about succeeding every time, it is about the opportunity to learn and get better. Don't be afraid to taste your dishes along the way, adjust the seasonings and serve accordingly.